ACTIVITY BANK

Sex Education

Judy Hunter

Sheila Phillips

Contents

How to use this book		3
Introduction		3

Activity

1	What we know, think and feel	4
2	Talking about sex	6
3	What's the difference?	8
4	Looking back, looking forward	10
5	My passport	12
6	Antennae	14
7	Storyboards	16
8	Who is it?	18
9	Put yourself on the line	20
10	Stepping into their shoes	22
11	I can choose to be assertive	24

Activity

12	My body, my feelings, my choice	26
13	Knowing the facts	28
14	What language shall we use?	30
15	Myth or truth?	32
16	Getting the message right	34
17	What have you heard?	36
18	Who's at risk?	38
19	Life choices	40
20	Dear Exxo Xtra Terrestrial	42
21	Who's out there?	44
	Appendix	46
	Skills matrix	48

Judy Hunter and Sheila Phillips come from an educational background and have wide experience in delivering training and producing resources for health education issues. They currently work with education and health professionals, business organisations and are trained counsellors.

Folens allows photocopying of pages marked 'copiable page' for educational use, providing that this use is within the confines of the purchasing institution. Copiable pages should not be declared in any return in respect of any photocopying licence.

Folens books are protected by international copyright laws. All rights are reserved. The copyright of all materials in this book, except where otherwise stated, remains the property of the publisher and authors. No part of this publication may be reproduced, stored in a retrieval system, or transmitted, in any form or by any means, for whatever purpose, without the written permission of Folens Limited.

This resource may be used in a variety of ways. However, it is not intended that teachers or children should write directly into the book itself.

Judy Hunter and Sheila Phillips hereby assert their moral rights to be identified as the authors of this work in accordance with the Copyright, Designs and Patents Act 1988.

Editor: Sue Harmes
Layout artist: Patricia Hollingsworth
Illustrations: Charmaine Peters. Bob Farley (Graham Cameron Illustration)

© 2000 Folens Limited, on behalf of the authors.

Every effort has been made to contact copyright holders of material used in this book. If any have been overlooked, we will be pleased to make any necessary arrangements.

First published 2000 by Folens Limited, Dunstable and Dublin.

Folens Limited, Albert House, Apex Business Centre, Boscombe Road, Dunstable, LU5 4RL, England.

ISBN 1 86202 566–5

Printed in Singapore by Craft Print.

How to use this book

There are 21 activities contained within this book. Each one has a teacher instruction page and a pupil activity page. The activities can be completed in short time slots or extended into longer periods, depending on the length of time you have available. They can also be differentiated to suit the needs of less able pupils. The activities can be presented in any order and you do not have to work your way right through the book. A matrix on page 48 provides a useful summary of, and reference to, the skills that pupils will learn through each activity, but we do recommend that Activity 1 and Activity 2 are presented as a starting point to your lessons.

Most of the activities in this book need few materials or resources other than copies of the activity sheet, paper and pens. They are designed to keep the teacher's workload to a minimum beyond planning how each activity will be carried out in the classroom. Most are designed so that pupils can work individually, in pairs or in small groups, depending on the teacher's preference. We recommend a balance of whole class, small group and individual work to provide pupils with plenty of opportunity to express their views, to listen and to try to understand the views of others and to develop communication and social skills.

The aims and expected outcomes of each activity are clearly indicated and the format for all activities is consistent to enable you quickly to feel comfortable and familiar with the style. All the information a teacher needs is contained here, not only to present the lesson confidently, but also to answer most questions that arise.

Introduction

Puberty is a crucial time in children's physical, emotional and sexual development. As they begin what is probably the most significant period of change and development in their lives, they take the first steps of their journey into adulthood as people with sexual feelings. They become aware of their emerging sexuality, and begin to develop values, beliefs and attitudes towards sex. Through working with pupils in the 11–16 age range, we have the opportunity to ensure they have an understanding of basic sexual health information and an opportunity to fully explore and discuss issues before they begin to place themselves at risk sexually and emotionally. Their background knowledge will vary enormously, depending on a school's policy, the attitudes and understanding of their parents and media influence.

Young people should grow into adulthood fully aware of the choices they can make and with an understanding that if and when they choose to be sexually active, this can bring intense pleasure and enjoyment, and fulfilment of a relationship. We want them not only to be aware of the many difficulties and dangers associated with sexual activity, but also to be able to celebrate their bodies and their sexuality.

Sex education should be an integral part of Personal, Social and Health Education programmes, developed with the aim of providing pupils with skills, knowledge and understanding to enable them to lead healthy and independent lives. Through work focused on raising and maintaining self-esteem, pupils should be enabled to feel that it is worth taking responsibility for their own well-being.

Schools need to consult with their governors and parents when they draw up their sex education policy, but beyond this, we recommend you involve parents as fully as possible as a means of support to the pupils. There is also much to be gained through involving outside agencies, not only as an additional resource in supporting the activities but also as a support for staff as they gain confidence and expertise in teaching sex education. Teachers will need to be aware of the sensitivities of the pupils' cultural and religious backgrounds when planning their lessons – some activities use explicit language and refer to sexual behaviour.

Activity 1 – Teacher's notes

What we know, think and feel

Establishing pupils' existing knowledge and understanding

AIMS

To establish the knowledge, understanding and attitudes of pupils towards sex to enable effective planning of the sex education lessons.

Teaching Points

- To be effective, sex education needs to be appropriate to the needs of pupils. This activity allows sex educators to gain an insight into pupils' thinking without influencing their perceptions in any way.
- Pupils should NOT write their names on the activity sheets. This enables pupils to feel free to express their true thoughts without fear of recrimination.
- Ensure pupils cannot see each other's work and give instructions that they should not share their work with anyone.
- The activity may be used alternatively as a basis for discussion.

USING THE ACTIVITY SHEET

The focus of the activity is to elicit the thoughts and attitudes of pupils, to enable you to plan sex education lessons effectively.

Step 1 Explain to the class that they are going to complete an activity in which you want them to be as honest as possible in sharing their thoughts. You will not ask them to write their names on the sheet, only to write whether they are male or female. Tell them that the purpose of the activity is to help identify the starting point for the whole class and that this will help you to plan their sex education lessons.

Step 2 As privately as possible, ask pupils to complete the activity sheet.

Step 3 Collect the sheets and thank the class for their help. Ask pupils if they have any questions or comments to make about the sex education lessons they will be having. Is there any topic in particular they wish to cover?

Step 4 The activity sheets can now be used to determine the thoughts and feelings of the class. Are there any marked differences between the boys' and the girls' comments? Do they give you an indication of what pupils think the reasons are for becoming sexually active? (Peer pressure? pleasure? curiosity? fear of a boyfriend or girlfriend ending the relationship?) This will give you an indication of the main issues to focus upon in subsequent lessons.

Extension Activities

- Invite pupils to draw up a list of things that people should think about before starting a sexual relationship.
- Using the activity sheet as a starting point, ask pupils to write a diary entry for the main speaker, explaining their feelings more fully.

Outcomes

- Raised awareness of pupils' thinking and attitudes towards sexual activity.
- Consideration of why people choose to have sex and the feelings associated with this.
- Initial exploration of pupils' attitudes and feelings in relation to sex.

Activity Sheet 1

What we know, think and feel

Please write below whether you are male or female. Do NOT write your name.

_____

Here are some pictures of two people talking. Fill in the blank speech bubbles, writing in what you think the person would be saying in response to the question 'Why?' and what they would be saying about how they felt.

If I had sex it would be because: _____

I think I would feel: _____

© Folens (copiable page)   ACTIVITY BANK: *Sex Education*

Activity 2 – Teacher's notes

Talking about sex

Setting the ground rules

AIMS

To establish ground rules for subsequent sex education lessons and provide the opportunity for the teacher to understand any particular sensitivities a pupil might have.

Teaching Points

- Setting ground rules involves the teacher as well as the pupils. Decide on the rules you want established and contribute these along with the class. You have rights too, and you will know what you need to help you feel comfortable.
- Explain to the class why it is important to have ground rules – so everyone feels as comfortable as possible with what is sometimes seen as a difficult topic to discuss.
- Encourage the class to think in positive rather than negative terms. In other words, you want to end up with a list of 'Dos' rather than 'Don'ts'. Ground rules might include 'treat everyone with respect', 'help everyone to feel as comfortable as possible' and 'consider other people's comments'.

USING THE ACTIVITY SHEET

The focus of the activity is to reach agreement on acceptable and non-acceptable behaviour during subsequent lessons.

Step 1 Divide the class into pairs or small groups. On a blank sheet of paper, ask each pair or group to list as many rules as they can think of that would help them to feel comfortable in class during their sex education lessons.

Step 2 Ask each pair or group to tell you one of their rules. Record each one. Keep going round each pair or group until everyone has contributed all the rules that they feel are important.

Step 3 Discuss any rules that need clarification. Add any of your own that you need. With the class, try to condense the list to no more than six golden rules. Remember, try to have 'do' not 'don't' rules.

Step 4 Ask pupils to complete the activity sheet individually. (You may like to look at these to check any area that is out of bounds for a pupil that you did not become aware of in the class discussion.)

Extension Activities

- Using the activity sheet, draw up a class statement about the ground rules you have agreed.
- Ask pupils to act out a scenario in which one of the rules outside the circle is taking place. Use this as a basis for class discussion as to why it is 'out of bounds'.

Outcomes

- Establishment of ground rules for pupil and teacher comfort and security.
- Increased teacher awareness of any specific sensitivities a pupil may have.

Activity Sheet 2

Talking about sex

You have decided as a class what the ground rules are going to be during your sex education lessons. Now you need to record these as a reminder to yourself. The diagram below shows a square which is an 'out of bounds' area and a circle in the middle which is 'within bounds'. Write in the circle what you have decided about how you will work together as a class. In the outer area (the square), write anything the class has decided will not be allowed. Finally, add your own thoughts about what is within the boundary and what is outside the boundary.

What I think about what is within the boundary _____

What I think about what is outside the boundary _____

© Folens (copiable page)   ACTIVITY BANK: *Sex Education*

Activity 3 – Teacher's notes

What's the difference?

Gender differences

AIMS

To explore gender differences, beginning with physical and developmental, and moving on to explore attitudinal and behavioural differences.

Teaching Points

- There are more than just physical differences between males and females.
- Discussing these differences and trying to understand them can help us in our relationships with each other.

USING THE ACTIVITY SHEET

The focus of the activity is to enable pupils to consider the attitudes, views and behaviours of the opposite sex.

Step 1   Working in small, single-gender groups, ask pupils to complete the 'Physical differences' sections of the activity sheet, listing physical differences between girls and boys (ignore the genital area). Differences that can be highlighted include body hair, muscle strength, depth of voice, size of hips and height.

Step 2   Review by inviting groups to contribute differences from their lists and write these on the board, adding any of your own.

Step 3   Now ask pupils to discuss any attitudinal differences, for example, likes and dislikes, pastimes, attitudes to school, parents, the future, type of career, the opposite sex. Take care to avoid stereotyping the sexes in terms of behaviour patterns (e.g. all boys are ...). Review by repeating Step 2.

Step 4   Invite pupils to complete the 'Attitude differences' sections on the activity sheet, selecting key points from the list you have compiled on the board.

Step 5   Invite the class to discuss the last sections on the activity sheet. This is in relation to trying to persuade the opposite sex to do things they do not want to do.

Step 6   Review and discuss. Were the boys or girls surprised by the views of the opposite sex? Do you think the views were accurate for you? Why or why not?

Step 7   Ask pupils to complete the final section of the activity sheet, according to what they feel are the key points.

Extension Activities

- Bring in extra support (another teacher, the school nurse, a health promotion officer) and work with boys and girls in different classrooms exploring any issues they feel it is easier to discuss in a single-sex forum.
- Debate a range of gender issues about sex such as possible differences in attitudes and responsibilities, with boys and girls formulating their thoughts and making notes initially in single-sex groups.

Outcomes

- An exploration beyond the more obvious gender differences and consideration of the attitudes and behaviours of the opposite sex in relation to a range of issues.
- Skill development in comparing and discussing.

Activity Sheet 3

What's the difference?

Discuss each of the following in your small groups, before completing according to what you feel are the main points.

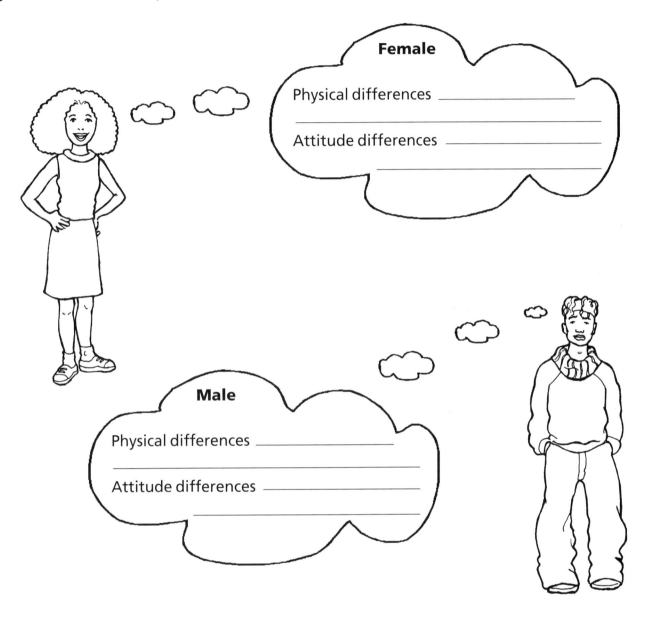

Female

Physical differences _____

Attitude differences _____

Male

Physical differences _____

Attitude differences _____

Things girls say to persuade boys

_____
_____
_____
_____
_____
_____

Things boys say to persuade girls

_____
_____
_____
_____
_____
_____

© Folens (copiable page)   ACTIVITY BANK: *Sex Education*

Activity 4 – Teacher's notes

Looking back, looking forward

Managing change, managing feelings

AIMS

To extend pupils' emotional language.
To raise awareness of possible future changes in their lives.

Teaching Points

- The emotional side of education is often neglected and yet it has a very significant part to play in sexual development.
- Many changes have happened to us so far in our lives and many changes will happen in the future.
- Feelings can change from one minute to the next and how we feel affects the decisions we make.
- It is important to consider how our feelings might change when we are making decisions about having a sexual relationship with someone. We can feel madly in love with someone one week and feel total dislike for them the next.
- Activity 9 provides further guidelines on how to set up a continuum in class.

USING THE ACTIVITY SHEET

The focus of the activity is to heighten awareness of the range of human feelings and how these feelings can change.

Step 1   Give some examples of 'feeling' words to the class before inviting pupils to think of as many of their own examples as they can in three minutes. This can be done as a whole class or in smaller groups. Collect the words on the board in an alphabetical list.

Step 2   To extend the range of feeling vocabulary, write some feeling continuums on the board and invite pupils to contribute feeling words that could be written at points on the continuum (e.g. furious – mildly irritated: words to place on the continuum might include angry, cross, mad, wild, enraged). Extend this activity by making a continuous line across the classroom (a rope may be used). Pupils can stand at the points on the line to indicate how they have felt at some time.

Step 3   Ask pupils to complete the first half of the activity sheet (Looking back), thinking particularly of significant events (moving house, changing schools, birth of a brother or sister).

Step 4   In a different colour, write in the feelings they remember experiencing alongside the event.

Step 5   Discuss with the class changes that are likely to happen to them in the future (leaving school, leaving home, getting a job, getting married and so on). Invite them to complete the second half of the activity sheet (Looking forward).

Step 6   Review by sharing some of these changes.

Extension Activities

- Using the activity sheet, ask pupils to think about changes to our bodies and write these in 'Looking back' and 'Looking forward'.
- Invite pupils to write a page from their diaries in five or ten or fifteen years' time, sharing something that is happening in their lives and how they feel about it.

Outcomes

- Extended emotional vocabulary.
- Increased awareness of how feelings affect decisions.
- Exploration of possible future changes in pupils' lives.

Activity Sheet 4

Looking back, looking forward

Looking back – try to think of some of the main changes that have happened in your life so far (moving house, changing schools, the birth of a new brother or sister).

Write them below as though you were looking back on them.

Using a different colour pen, now mark on the feelings you remember experiencing alongside the changes.

Looking forward – try to imagine some of the changes that are likely to happen in your life in the future. Write them below as though you were looking forward.

Using a different colour pen, now mark on the feelings you might experience alongside the changes.

© Folens (copiable page)   ACTIVITY BANK: *Sex Education*   11

Activity 5 – Teacher's notes

My passport

I am unique, I have my own qualities

AIMS

To highlight individuality and self-esteem.

Teaching Points

Material needed
Pupils to bring in a photo of themselves (optional).

- Everyone is unique. Everyone has individual trade marks, individual skills, strengths and qualities.
- Sometimes it feels good to be different from everyone else (e.g. when we achieve something through a particular talent and feel proud of it) and sometimes it feels better to be seen as the same as everyone else (e.g. when we meet new people and want to fit in with them because it feels comfortable).
- There are some situations when it is difficult to be seen as different.

USING THE ACTIVITY SHEET

The focus of the activity is to explore how everyone is unique, special and has different skills and qualities.

Step 1 Discuss with pupils what being individual means. When does it feel good to be different from everyone else, when does it feel better to be seen as the same as everyone else? What are the situations and times when it is difficult to be different, to have a different view, to make a different choice from other people?

Step 2 Ask the class – what is a skill? (Something that we can do or can learn to do, such as the skills of communicating, decision making, problem solving, negotiating, assertion.) What is a quality? (Some trait within ourselves that we have or can try to develop such as patience, tolerance, honesty, sensitivity, loyalty.)

Step 3 Build up a range of words for skills and qualities in two lists on the board.

Step 4 Ask pupils to complete the activity sheet individually.

Step 5 Review by inviting pupils either in small groups or as a whole class to share the final element of their activity sheet – their trade mark or special skill or quality.

Extension Activities

- Develop a group or class trade mark.
- Invite pupils to design a poster that advertises the strengths, skills and qualities of the class.

Outcomes

- Self-esteem and confidence building.
- Heightened awareness of the notion of individuality.

Activity Sheet 5

My passport

Name _____

Date of birth _____

Hair colour _____

Eye colour _____

Likes _____
_____
_____
_____
_____
_____

Dislikes _____
_____
_____
_____
_____
_____

Skills _____
_____
_____
_____
_____
_____

Qualities _____
_____
_____
_____
_____
_____

Greatest achievement _____
_____
_____

Distinguishing skill, quality or talent _____
_____

Activity 6 – Teacher's notes

Antennae

Informed decision making

AIMS

To encourage pupils to use their senses and reflect on their thoughts and feelings before making choices.

Teaching Points

- It is useful in our relationships to try to see and evaluate things from other people's point of view.
- Perceptions are not necessarily right or wrong – they may be different according to how we view the world.
- It can be helpful to use our perceptions and our senses to be alert to potentially difficult situations.

USING THE ACTIVITY SHEET

The focus of the activity is to encourage pupils to use as much information as possible before making choices.

Step 1 Ask the class to look at the picture at the top of the activity sheet – what do they see? If you look closely you can see either a rabbit or a duck lying on its back, depending upon your perception.

Step 2 Ask pupils to try to imagine themselves in the three scenarios you are going to read out. After reading each one, ask the pupils (individually or in small groups) to complete the activity sheet by considering what their perceptions are of the situation ('this might turn into a very tricky situation'), what other people might say in that situation ('come on, it will be fine'), what they might feel (excited, scared, wanted) and what they would know that might influence them (knowledge about sexually transmitted infections).

The three scenarios are:
1. You are at a party with a group of your best friends. You have paired up with someone you have been attracted to for ages and you are really happy about it. This person asks if you will leave the party and go to her or his house, which is empty, so you can be alone.
2. You have been going out with someone for about six months. You both decide you want to have sex together for the first time but your partner doesn't want to use a condom.
3. You overhear a group of people discussing a friend of yours. Someone says they saw your friend coming out of the local GU (Genito-Urinary) clinic. The group discusses how often your friend has been off school recently and how ill they look. Someone says they heard your friend was HIV positive.

Step 3 Share the answers of the class. Focus particularly on the final question on the activity sheet ('What would I do?') by asking pupils why they came to that conclusion. Point out the range of different responses and the importance of being able to see things from a different point of view.

Extension Activities

- Ask pupils, in groups, to role-play the three situations with their own endings. Review these endings in a class discussion.
- Ask the pupils to devise more scenarios to bring in other PSHE issues.

Outcomes

- Increased awareness of the advantage of carefully considering difficult situations from all angles.
- Increased awareness that everyone is responsible for their own choices and decisions.

Activity Sheet 6

Antennae

We all see things differently from each other, we all have different perceptions.

What do you see here?

Try to imagine yourself in the three scenarios your teacher is going to read out. For each one, write below what your perceptions are of the situation ('what do I see?'), what people might say to try to influence you ('what do I hear?'), what are your feelings ('what do I feel?'), and what you know that might influence you ('what do I think?'). After each one, write down what you would do after considering all of the above.

what do I see?   what do I hear?   what do I feel?   what do I think?   what would I do?

scenario 1
- what do I see? _____
- what do I hear? _____
- what do I feel? _____
- what do I think? _____
- what would I do? _____

scenario 2
- what do I see? _____
- what do I hear? _____
- what do I feel? _____
- what do I think? _____
- what would I do? _____

scenario 3
- what do I see? _____
- what do I hear? _____
- what do I feel? _____
- what do I think? _____
- what would I do? _____

© Folens (copiable page)   ACTIVITY BANK: *Sex Education*

Activity 7 – Teacher's notes

Storyboards

The consequences of the decisions we make

AIMS

To increase awareness of personal responsibility for decisions and how these decisions have consequences.

Teaching Points

- This is an opportunity for pupils to focus on their own decision-making skills – try to resist the temptation to influence the process.
- Encourage ideas for a range of possible alternatives for the ending to the scenario(s) you will read out.
- Individuals can be responsible for making their own choices in relation to their sexuality and sexual health and it is important to consider the possible consequences of those choices.

USING THE ACTIVITY SHEET

The focus of the activity is to highlight the fact that everyone can make their own choices and these choices will result in different outcomes.

Step 1 Explain to the class that you are going to read out the beginning of a film script. As yet, there is no ending to this script. Ask pupils to imagine they are directing the film and must decide on three possible endings, depending on the decisions made by characters in the film.

Step 2 Read the following scenario to the class: 'A group of teenage girls are staying at Nadine's house for a sleepover. Nadine's parents will not be back until at least midnight. Word went round school that a party was taking place and a group of boys who the girls know well have now turned up. An hour later the party is going well and at about 10.30pm, Matthew and Justine ask Nadine if they can go into one of the bedrooms.' (Now read once more.)

Step 3 Ask the class to complete the activity sheet. This is best done by splitting the class into small groups to discuss the different endings but can be completed individually if you prefer.

Step 4 Follow up: in a plenary session, invite the class to share the ending they chose as the one most likely to happen and their reasons for this. Ask them to consider whether the outcomes were good or bad, healthy or harmful, and for whom. Discuss what can influence decisions and what makes some decisions difficult to make (e.g. our feelings).

Extension Activities

- The activity sheet can be photocopied and more scenarios presented as appropriate to the class and the issues you are trying to raise (e.g. an unwanted pregnancy due to having unprotected sex).
- Split the class into groups and ask them to devise scenarios which involve difficult decisions. Collect them in and redistribute around the class inviting groups to write possible endings.

Outcomes

- Increased responsibility for making decisions about moral choices. These choices may be between good and bad, healthy and harmful, safe and dangerous, and may include saying 'no'.
- Increased awareness that everyone needs to consider the possible consequences of their decisions on themselves, their families and friends.

Activity Sheet 7

Storyboards

In the boxes below, write very briefly three possible endings to the scenario.
In each box also write the reasons why each scene ended in this way.

Ending 1

The story ends by ...

The reasons it ended this way were ...

Ending 2

The story ends by ...

The reasons it ended this way were ...

Ending 3

The story ends by ...

The reasons it ended this way were ...

The ending which I think would be most likely to happen is _____

because _____

© Folens (copiable page)   ACTIVITY BANK: *Sex Education*   17

Activity 8 – Teacher's notes

Who is it?

Exploring perceptions of people and situations

AIMS

To increase awareness that attitudes and beliefs are often determined by our perceptions.
To develop problem-solving skills.

Teaching Points

- We all have different perceptions about people and situations.
- We all have different questions, feelings and confusions about our sexual development and sexuality.
- This activity can be adapted for other situations where you want to build up a picture of a person.
- This activity may need careful handling to avoid disruptive or negative comments about issues of sexuality (e.g. homosexuality).

USING THE ACTIVITY SHEET

The focus of the activity is to explore pupils' perceptions, attitudes and beliefs towards different situations through characters that are relevant and credible to them.

Step 1 Draw an outline of a genderless person on the board, sketching in a symbol for the brain and a symbol for the heart (as shown on the activity sheet).

Step 2 Give pupils two pieces of information about the character you have drawn, for example, 'This is someone who is 13 and who is pregnant.'

Step 3 Ask the class for further information about the person and write this in or around the character. Do they look happy? What is the person thinking and feeling? What is their family or personal lifestyle? Are they confused about their sexual development?

Step 4 Now use the character as a focus for discussion. What could be done to help them? What would you say to them? (Encourage pupils to make only positive suggestions.)

Step 5 Ask pupils to complete the activity sheet by building up a character of their own. On the board, write some examples of pieces of information they could use as a starting point (e.g. a girl who is pregnant; someone who is worried they have HIV; someone whose partner wants to have sex with them; someone whose friends call them names because of their sexual behaviour). Pupils can then choose two pieces of information for their character.

Step 6 Review by inviting pupils to share some of the information about their characters, and particularly to share what they think the person should do about their situation.

Extension Activities

- Invite the pupils to build up pictures of people who are part of the character's lives (parent, friend, teacher, partner).
- Invite some of the pupils to take on the role of the characters and invite the rest of the class to ask questions of the characters to find out more about them.

Outcomes

- Exploration of perceptions, attitudes and beliefs.
- Problem solving in relation to how to help the character(s).
- Developing skills of empathy.

Activity Sheet 8

Who is it?

Write below the two pieces of information you have chosen about the character.

1. _____

2. _____

Write more information in and around the character, according to what you think this character might be like. What does this person look like? What is this person thinking? What is this person feeling? Who is in this person's family? What are their hobbies? Where do they go socially? Are they still at school or do they have a job? How old are they? Draw in their face if you can.

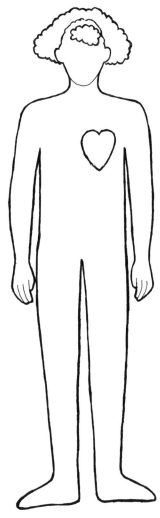

What do you think this person should do because of the situation they are in?

_____

_____

Activity 9 – Teacher's notes

Put yourself on the line

Exploring attitudes and beliefs

AIMS

To encourage pupils to explore their attitudes and the attitudes of others in relation to sexual health matters.

Teaching Points

- This activity can be done in two ways. Pupils can either place a cross along the continuums according to where they stand on a given topic, or
- You can set this up in a more experiential way by making two ends of the classroom symbolise the two ends of the continuum. Pupils then place themselves along the continuum according to their views. Go along the continuum and randomly ask pupils along the line what their views are. Pupils can then reshuffle themselves so they are grouped in line with other people's attitudes.

USING THE ACTIVITY SHEET

The focus of the activity is to stimulate pupils to think more deeply about the views they hold.

Step 1 Provide some general examples of continuums for pupils, making the two opposite ends fairly extreme. Explain that the purpose of the continuum is to help them consider where they would place themselves along the continuum, according to their views of the given topics. A possible example could be the argument for and against smoking in public places.

Step 2 Ask pupils to complete the activity sheet by placing a cross on the continuums according to their views.

Step 3 Invite pupils, either writing down individually or discussing in groups, to express their views – for which statements did they hold similar views to each other? For which statements did they hold different views from each other?

Step 4 Review the activity with the class by asking groups to share any statements about which they held fairly different views within the group and discuss these with the whole class.

Extension Activities

- To make this into a debating activity, split the group in half according to where they have placed themselves on the continuum(s), then ask them to debate the merits of their position and try to persuade people to 'join the other side'.
- Ask pupils to bring in a range of newspapers and magazines and use them to identify letters, articles and headlines where the writer obviously has firm views on contentious issues. Do they agree or disagree? Ask them to choose a topic about which to write a letter.

Outcomes

- Increased awareness and expression of attitudes and beliefs.
- Increased awareness of the need to listen to and respect another person's viewpoint.
- Development of persuasive argument debating skills.

Activity Sheet 9

Put yourself on the line

Place a cross on the continuums below, according to your view on the given topics.

| The age of sexual consent should be raised to 21. | There should be no age of consent. It should be a free choice. |

_____

| HIV/Aids is a disease only homosexuals get. | Anyone at all can get HIV/Aids. It is just down to bad luck. |

_____

| Schools should not teach any form of sex education. | Schools should teach everything about sex as explicitly as possible. |

_____

| Anyone who is still a virgin by the age of 25 must have something wrong with him or her. | If people choose never to have sex that is fine. It is their choice. |

_____

| A very high number of people who have sex for the first time when they are drunk regret it later. | It would not make any difference if someone had drunk alcohol or not. Their decision would be the same. |

_____

| Contraceptives should be more freely available to young people. | The availability of contraceptives needs to be tightly controlled. People should only be able to get them from their doctor. |

_____

| Parents should be much stricter with their children to make sure they do not have under-age sex. | Parents should just leave their children alone. It is their decision whether to have sex or not. |

_____

ACTIVITY BANK: *Sex Education*

Activity 10 – Teacher's notes

Stepping into their shoes

Understanding other people's beliefs

AIMS

To encourage pupils to become more aware of other people's beliefs and cultures and to develop an understanding of why other people may hold the views they do.

Teaching Points

- We cannot always tell by looking at someone what they are like and what their beliefs are.
- Knowing more about the views of others can help us work out our own.
- It is OK for someone to have beliefs that are different from our own.
- Trying to understand why people hold the beliefs they do can help us build better relationships.
- Sometimes we don't even know what we really believe until we have had the opportunity to think about it.
- A person's views can change.
- This activity covers a broad topic and may be extended over two lessons.

USING THE ACTIVITY SHEET

The focus of the activity is to stimulate pupils to think more deeply about both their views and beliefs and those of others.

Step 1 Introduce the activity to pupils by writing on the board general categories of groups of people according to set criteria. For example, according to their ages.

Step 2 Which categories would agree or disagree with the statement 'There is far too much talk these days about sex.'? Why is this? Is there anything that might cause the groupings of people to change their views?

Step 3 You can extend this into groupings and statements of your choice. It can, for example, be a very useful activity to focus on different religions if you would like to raise this as a topic. (Present pupils with statements and ask them to attach them to one of the faiths that you have listed on the board – a Hindu could not marry a Christian; a Muslim could not marry a Jew, and so on.)

Step 4 Read out the statements from page 47 and ask pupils to indicate on their activity sheet which statement belongs to which person by writing a, b, c, and so on next to the pictures. There are no right or wrong answers – just different perceptions of the examples given.

Step 5 Review by inviting the class to share who they thought the different statements belonged to. Why did they think the people owned the statements they chose? What might influence those people to change their view about something? Explain the concept of empathy and ask pupils to write down which viewpoint they empathised with the most and why. Share results in a class discussion.

Extension Activities

- Ask pupils to imagine they are one of the people on the activity sheet – what views do they hold?
- Ask pupils to imagine they are journalists with the brief to interview someone about their beliefs – ask them to prepare the questions they will ask.

Outcomes

- Developing empathy through increased awareness and understanding of other people's views.
- Exploration of own thoughts and beliefs through discussion and reflection.

Activity Sheet 10

Stepping into their shoes

Ten statements are going to be read out to you. Decide who you think each statement belongs to and write the matching letter (a to j) in the box provided. Under the last two pictures write your own description of the people shown.

Nurse, aged 30, married, one son

Bank manager, aged 38, divorced, two children

Police officer, aged 29, lives with partner

Journalist, aged 26, single

Social worker, aged 32, lives with partner

Solicitor, aged 44, married, three children

Judge, aged 62, married, four children

Doctor, aged 28, single

Farmer, aged 56, second marriage, no children

Car salesperson, aged 21, married

© Folens (copiable page)   ACTIVITY BANK: *Sex Education*   23

Activity 11 – Teacher's notes

I can choose to be assertive

Practising assertive behaviour

AIMS

To enable pupils to reflect on their thoughts, feelings and attitudes when experiencing different behaviours, particularly assertiveness.

Teaching Points

- Being assertive does not mean being aggressive.
- Being assertive means staying calm and not only being firm about what you want but also acknowledging the rights of others.
- Assertive behaviour is a skill that we can all learn through practice.
- Being assertive can help you in difficult situations, particularly when someone is trying to get you to do something you do not want to do.
- Being passive means accepting the situation you are in without question.

USING THE ACTIVITY SHEET

The focus of the activity is for pupils to experience what assertive behaviour is and reflect on how and when they could use it.

Step 1 Ask pupils to work in pairs and decide who is partner A and who is partner B. Give them the following instructions:
Partner A – "Ask the person you are sitting with to do something for you (e.g. your homework), or lend you something (e.g. some music), or tell you something (e.g. a secret). Try to make it something realistic. You are going to really try to persuade the other person to let you have your own way. You can ask for what you want as many times as you like, in whatever way you like, but do not use any physically threatening behaviour."
Partner B – "Whatever your partner asks you to do, you must refuse. You can refuse in whatever way you choose, as many times as you choose, but do not use any physically threatening behaviour."

Step 2 Start the activity. Stop after one minute. Ask partner A from each pair to swap places with a partner A from another pair. Repeat the activity and repeat Step 2 several times.

Step 3 Now ask partners A and B to swap roles and repeat several times.

Step 4 Ask pupils to complete question 1 on the activity sheet. Then review by discussing pupils' feelings and reactions to the activity. From the discussion, clarify what assertive behaviour is.

Step 5 Ask pupils to work in pairs on questions 2 and 3 of the activity sheet. Assess the advantages and disadvantages of each kind of behaviour.

Extension Activities

- Brainstorm on flip-chart paper, 'assertive behaviour', 'non-assertive behaviour', 'aggressive' behaviour. Further clarify differences between the behaviours.
- Ask pupils to devise scenarios where it might be difficult to be assertive and discuss and practise possible responses.

Outcomes

- Better understanding of the relative advantages and disadvantages of assertive behaviour.
- Acknowledgement of how another person's behaviour, passive or aggressive, can influence our own.

Activity Sheet 11

I can choose to be assertive

1. Think back to the activity you have just done in pairs, then answer the following questions:

   What did it feel like when someone said 'no' to you?

   _____

   What did it feel like saying 'no' to someone?

   _____

   What helped you to believe that someone really meant 'no'?

   _____

Assertive behaviour is about being firm and clear about what you want. It does not mean you need to be aggressive.

2. In pairs, practise some assertive responses to the following. Take it in turns to go first.

   – A group of friends persuading you to have a party when your parents are on holiday.

   – A group in school teasing you about being a virgin.

   – A partner pressurising you to have sex.

   – An older brother or sister who wants you to lie to your parents about him or her stopping at a friend's house.

   – A close friend who wants you to make up a foursome and you don't want to go.

3. Now do the same exercise using passive and then aggressive responses.

© Folens (copiable page)   ACTIVITY BANK: *Sex Education*

Activity 12 – Teacher's notes

My body, my feelings, my choice

Rights and responsibilities in relation to sexuality, age and other areas of differentiation

AIMS

To allow pupils to explore what rights they have in relation to their sexuality and to develop an appreciation that rights bring with them responsibilities.

Teaching Points

- Many people believe that we can make our own choices about our sexuality, our bodies and our feelings.
- It is important to respect that everyone has the right to make their own choices.
- These choices are irrespective of whether you are male or female, what age or group you belong to: you always have the right to make your own choices.

USING THE ACTIVITY SHEET

The focus of the activity is to heighten awareness of the view that everyone has rights in relation to their bodies and their sexuality and these rights should be respected.

Step 1 Explore with the class the meaning of 'sexuality' by gathering different viewpoints on a definition for it. Contribute any aspects that are missing in the pupil definitions. (It is also about being happy, being you, being the sex you are and choosing to be sexually active or not.)

Step 2 Divide the class into single sex groups. On the board, make two separate headings 'male' and 'female' and ask pupils to complete the following statements under the appropriate headings: As a girl/boy I can; As a girl/boy I cannot; If I were a boy/girl I could not; As a teenager I can ... and so on. This is designed to help pupils think about restrictions they place on themselves.

Step 3 Review and discuss by inviting pupils to share some of their responses. In the same groups, ask pupils to discuss the Declaration of Rights on the activity sheet, particularly focusing on whether it applies to themselves.

Step 4 Review the Declaration of Rights by discussing the following with the class:
Are there any statements that they feel apply only to one sex? Are there any statements that they feel apply more to one sex than the other? Is there any statement that they feel is not a right? Is there any statement which they feel should be added to the Declaration of Rights?

Step 5 Ask pupils to complete the two questions at the bottom of the activity sheet individually. Check round the class to see which statements were chosen – why were those statements in particular chosen? What would help to make it easier to keep those rights and responsibilities?

Extension Activities

- As a class, discuss the different names given to girls and boys who are sexually active (e.g. girls may be 'slags' and boys 'studs') and look at the implications for how they treat each other.
- Draw up a Declaration of Rights for being members of this class and display it on the wall.

Outcomes

- Increased awareness of rights and responsibilities in relation to 'my body and my sexuality'.
- Increased awareness of the restrictions other people place upon themselves.

Activity Sheet 12

My body, my feelings, my choice

Consider the Declaration of Rights below. Are there any that you feel do not apply to you?

Declaration of Rights

- I have the right to be treated with respect.
- I have the right to express my feelings.
- I have the right to my own opinions.
- I have the right to feel safe.
- I have the right to say 'yes' and 'no'.
- I have the right to state my own needs.
- I have the right to make mistakes.
- I have the right not to be pressured.
- I have the right to ask for what I want.
- I have the right to do what I want with my body.

Which right or responsibility do you feel is the most difficult to keep to?

Why do you think it is the most difficult?

© Folens (copiable page)   ACTIVITY BANK: *Sex Education*

Activity 13 – Teacher's notes

Knowing the facts

The terminology used to describe the sexual organs

AIMS

To ensure all pupils have basic knowledge about the outer male and female sexual organs, and understand the associated terminology.

Teaching Points

- This activity should NOT be used as a test.
- Pupils need to hear the words, and to see them written down with their correct spelling.
- You may find the guide on page 46 useful when explaining some of the body parts and their function to pupils.

USING THE ACTIVITY SHEET

The focus of the activity is to ensure all pupils have seen, heard and written the biological terminology used to describe the sexual organs.

Step 1 Explain to pupils that you are going to clarify the correct biological terminology used to describe the sexual organs. Then ask them to write the words on the diagrams given on the activity sheet.

Step 2 Write the name of each of the sexual organs on the board, instructing pupils where to write each of the words on their diagrams. Describe the function of each organ as you work through the diagrams.

Step 3 Using the words now written on their diagrams, ask pupils to fill in the gaps in the sentences written below the diagrams.

Step 4 Read out the correct words that should be written in the sentences, allowing pupils time to make any corrections on their sheets.

Extension Activities

- Discuss why it is important to know the biological terminology in a sex education programme.
- Ask pupils, in pairs, to discuss how much they have learned in the lesson, which parts they found easy and difficult and why.

Outcomes

- A common understanding within the class of the biological terminology used to describe the sexual organs and the function of those organs.
- Coming to terms with some of the inhibitions and embarrassments pupils may have towards biological matters of sex. This will facilitate more open discussion in future lessons.

Activity Sheet 13

Knowing the facts

Label the diagrams shown below of the male and female sexual organs.
The sentences underneath the diagrams describe what some of the different sexual organs do. In the gaps, fill in the name of the sexual organ described.

The Male
(as seen from the side,
externally and internally)

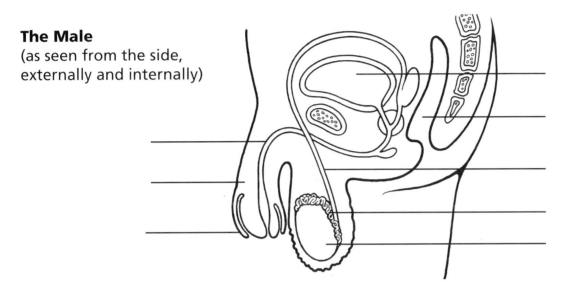

The _____ becomes erect so that it can fit into a female's vagina. The _____ make sperm cells. The _____ protects the sensitive part of the penis. The _____ stores urine. The _____ is a sac containing two testes.

The Female
(as seen from
below, externally)

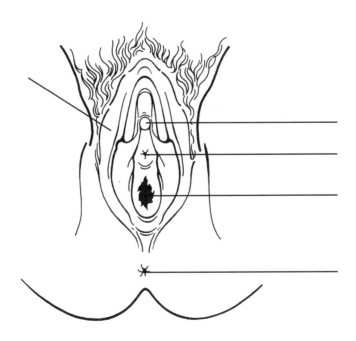

The _____ is an opening leading to the internal sex organs. The _____ are the lips of the vagina. The _____ is a small pea-like structure and is a very sensitive organ. The _____ is an opening through which a female passes urine.

© Folens (copiable page)   ACTIVITY BANK: *Sex Education*

Activity 14 – Teacher's notes

What language shall we use?

Distinguishing between appropriate and inappropriate language

AIMS

To establish the sexual language that will be acceptable in class.
To highlight the appropriateness or inappropriateness of language in different situations.

Teaching Points

- Pupils need to see, hear and write the appropriate terminology to avoid embarrassment that might be caused by its misuse.
- It is important not to criticise any of the vocabulary pupils might use elsewhere (unless it is used in an abusive or insulting way), but simply to acknowledge that this might be different from the language that will be acceptable in class. It may take pupils a minute or so to overcome initial embarrassment, so give them plenty of encouragement and reassurance.
- This is a useful point in a sex education programme to encourage parental involvement by inviting parents to teach pupils a common language prior to the start of the lessons. You could send parents a copy of the information box on page 47.

USING THE ACTIVITY SHEET

The focus of the activity is to ensure pupils understand and can use an acceptable sexual language in class and in other situations.

Step 1 Divide the class into six groups, two groups A, two groups B and two groups C.

Step 2 Ask groups A to write down as many words or phrases as they can think of for the female sexual organs, groups B the male sexual organs and groups C the sexual act. Emphasise that they can include any slang words at all that they have heard or seen written.

Step 3 After two to three minutes, swap the sheets of paper around so that groups A have the papers from groups B, and so on. Ask them to add any words or phrases they can think of that have not already been written.

Step 4 Acknowledge words and phrases by holding up the sheets. It is advisable, however, NOT to read out the slang words. This could be seen as inappropriate language for a teacher to use if taken out of the context of the activity.

Step 5 Tell the class they are now going to set aside all the slang words and other language that they thought of and explain to them the terminology that is appropriate. You may find the terminology on page 47 useful.

Step 6 Ask the pupils to complete activity sheets individually. Make sure you remove papers with slang words or clean any boards.

Extension Activities

- Distribute slips of paper and invite pupils to write down any questions they would like to ask. Reassure them that no one will know who has written which question. Use the questions to make your own list of the points that need clarifying in the next lesson.
- Hold a class discussion of why slang words can be offensive and inappropriate.

Outcomes

- Common understanding and clarity of an acceptable and appropriate sexual language.

Activity Sheet 14

What language shall we use?

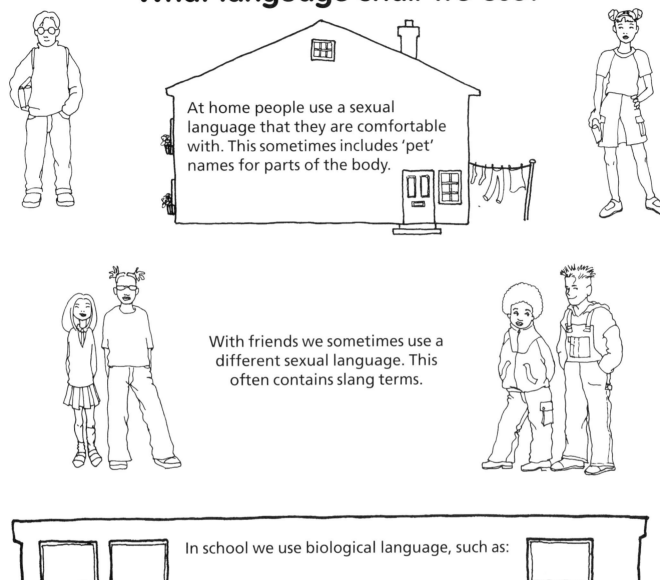

At home people use a sexual language that they are comfortable with. This sometimes includes 'pet' names for parts of the body.

With friends we sometimes use a different sexual language. This often contains slang terms.

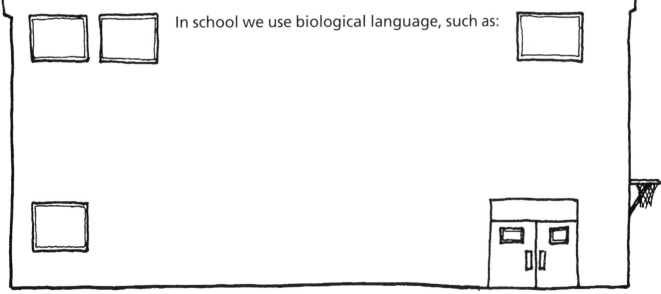

In school we use biological language, such as:

You may find it useful to use the biological language we use in school, if you ever need to talk to a doctor, nurse or other adult. It can be less embarrassing and means you can be clearly understood.

Activity 15 – Teacher's notes

Myth or truth?
Dispelling the myths

AIMS

To encourage pupils to consider some myths in relation to sex and think beyond them to judge if they are generally true.

Teaching Points

- People often hold myths which they come to think of as being true. We need to think about them and decide if they are true or just a myth.
- If we think something is not true and someone tries to convince us otherwise, we should check it with someone who will know the answer. Never be afraid to ask questions about sex, as finding out accurate information can help to keep us safe. (Use Activity 21 as a follow up to make sure pupils know who to approach for help or to discuss examples from it in the context of this activity.)

USING THE ACTIVITY SHEET

The focus of the activity is to dispel some possible myths about sex and to encourage pupils to think more deeply about what might be true and untrue.

Step 1   Read out each of the following 'myths'. Pupils can work in small groups to discuss each statement and say whether it is true or false, before moving to whole class discussion: it always snows at Christmas; all politicians are liars; you don't get anywhere in sport without taking drugs; all teenagers are moody; all parents are bad-tempered; men are stronger than women; men don't cry.

Step 2   Ask pupils to consider some more myths by completing the activity sheet either individually or in pairs.

Step 3   Read out the correct answers to the activity sheet: 1. False 2. False 3. True 4. False 5. False 6. True or False 7. True 8. False 9. True 10. True.

Step 4   Discuss any statements which the class felt did not have a very clear-cut answer, for example, question 6. Why was this? Are there any other myths they have heard of in relation to sex or any statements they are not absolutely sure are true or false? (Some clarification for question 2 – semen released before ejaculation could cause pregnancy if the penis comes into contact with the vagina, and question 5 – a girl can conceive at first ovulation, which will be before her first period.)

Extension Activities

- Ask pupils to explore what makes us believe something which is not true, and why so many myths persist. In pairs, they could take one of the 'myths' and try to convince the rest of the class that it is true. A vote could be taken for and against. Discuss what caused people to vote the way they did.
- Invite pupils to look at some possible assertive responses to use when people are trying to convince us that something is true when we really believe it isn't.

Outcomes

- Examining the causes behind some of the beliefs we hold.
- Making an informed choice on whether something is true or untrue.

Activity Sheet 15

Myth or truth?

Answer the questions by putting in a tick (✓) for 'true' and a cross (✗) for 'false'.

1. A woman cannot become pregnant if she has sexual intercourse while standing up.

2. A woman cannot become pregnant if the man does not ejaculate.

3. Different forms of contraception have different reliability rates.

4. A woman cannot become pregnant the first time she has sexual intercourse.

5. A woman cannot become pregnant if she has not started her periods.

6. Girls want a relationship — boys want sex.

7. Nature has programmed us to want to have sex to ensure the human race continues.

8. Hormones are just an excuse for bad moods in teenagers.

9. Under 16s can get contraceptives from clinics.

10. Girls who have sex under 16 run a higher risk of cancer of the cervix later in life.

© Folens (copiable page)   ACTIVITY BANK: *Sex Education*

Activity 16 – Teacher's notes

Getting the message right
Developing understanding of sex education issues

AIMS

To develop knowledge and understanding of sex education issues affecting pupils through designing an advertising campaign for younger pupils.

Teaching Points

Materials needed
Information leaflets and books on various aspects of sex education.

- A useful sex education strategy is to involve pupils in planning an activity for pupils slightly younger than themselves. This distances some of the issues, often making it easier to explore them.
- By identifying and clarifying information for younger pupils, they are extending their own knowledge, engaging in discussion with their peers and closely examining sex education resources.

USING THE ACTIVITY SHEET

The focus of the activity is to explore the medium of advertising in order to develop further knowledge and understanding of sex education.

Step 1 Discuss with pupils the range of advertising methods (leaflets, television, radio, cinema, magazines, newspapers, billboards), and write them on the board. Which do they think are most successful in reaching and engaging interest from young people?

Step 2 Explain that advertising has to have a specific purpose – to change someone's behaviour or make them buy something. Tell pupils that they are going to design an advertisement about a sex education issue for pupils one year younger than themselves. What kind of information do they think pupils need? (What happens when a girl starts having periods, what are wet dreams, how do people's bodies change during puberty?) Collect their ideas on the board.

Step 3 Divide the class into small groups and give each one a different topic to consider (e.g. safer sex or puberty issues or contraception). Each group can decide on or be assigned a different advertising medium.

Step 4 Make available any resources you have collected to help pupils decide what information they need. (Health Promotion Departments may help to provide these.)

Step 5 Ask pupils to record key points about their advertising campaign on the activity sheet.

Extension Activities

- Invite pupils to devise campaigns to inform other groups of people, e.g. parents (how to talk to your children about sex), or teachers (what young people need from sex education lessons).
- If appropriate, materials produced can be 'tested' on a younger audience so that pupils receive feedback on the impact of their advertisement.

Outcomes

- Consolidation of knowledge around sex education issues, according to your choice(s) of topics.
- Increased awareness of the impact of the media and the methods used to influence people.

Activity Sheet 16

Getting the message right

Which advertising form have you decided to use?

_____

_____

Why have you chosen this particular method?

_____

_____

What is the purpose of the message?

_____

_____

What are the main messages you are aiming to convey in your advertisement?

_____

_____

On the back of the sheet, briefly outline below the advertisement you have devised:

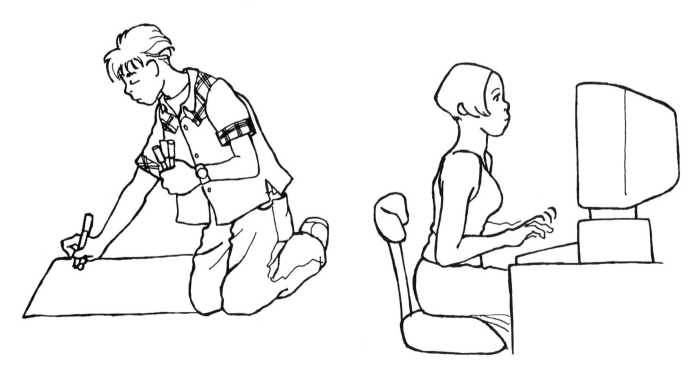

© Folens (copiable page) ACTIVITY BANK: *Sex Education*

Activity 17 –Teacher's notes

What have you heard?

The facts about HIV

AIMS

To consider the truths and untruths about Human Immunodeficiency Virus (HIV) by enabling pupils to ask questions in a safe and comfortable way.

Teaching Points

Materials needed
Literature or leaflets about HIV and AIDS.

◆ The concept of the activity is to develop an accurate understanding of what HIV is and how it can be transmitted.
◆ The answers to any questions about HIV and AIDS can be found in health leaflets (see your Health Promotion Department). Further information to help you can also be found on page 47.
◆ Don't be afraid to say you don't know the answer to any question – this could be the focus of an investigation by the pupils using any literature you have available.

USING THE ACTIVITY SHEET

The focus of the activity is to gather as much information as possible about HIV and consider whether statements about HIV are true or untrue.

Step 1 Ask the pupils to write as many statements as they can about HIV and AIDS on separate slips of paper. Tell pupils they do not have to decide if the statements are true or untrue, they are simply writing down anything they have heard or read. (Examples of possible statements might be: you can catch HIV from toilet seats, you can catch it if someone spits at you, you cannot catch HIV unless you are gay.) At this point tell pupils that if they have a question about HIV or AIDS, they can also add it to the first statement, for example, 'You can get it from sharing a toothbrush.' The aim is to generate as many statements as possible. You could add some yourself.

Step 2 Collect in all the statements and shuffle them. Divide the class into small groups and give each group a pile of statements.

Step 3 Ask pupils to record on the activity sheet the categories the group thinks each statement fits into. (True, False or Don't know.) If a group cannot agree on a categorisation of a statement they should put it into the Don't know category.

Step 4 Discuss the statements with the class by going round the groups checking the True and False statements are correctly categorised and clarify the Don't know statements.

Extension Activities

◆ As a class or in groups produce an information sheet on HIV and AIDS which clarifies the points pupils think are especially important.
◆ Discuss with the class how the media portrays people who are HIV positive and collect any relevant cuttings from magazines and newspapers.

Outcomes

◆ Increased knowledge of the facts relating to HIV and AIDS.
◆ Clarification of some of the misconceptions about HIV and AIDS.

What have you heard?

Activity Sheet 17

Discuss with your group which statements you think are TRUE and which ones are FALSE. Write these inside the appropriate ribbon. If there are any statements that you cannot agree are either true or false, write these inside the ribbon marked DON'T KNOW.

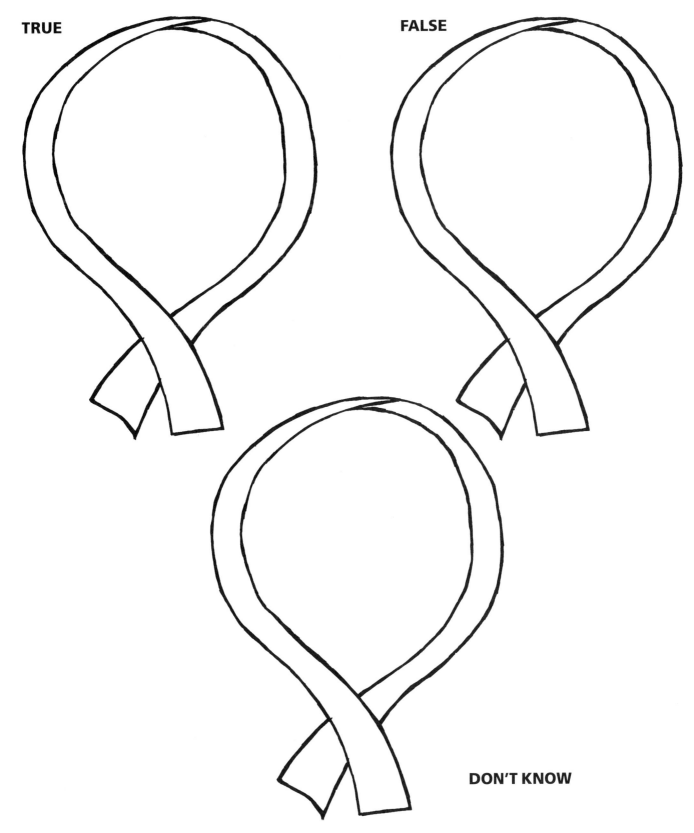

© Folens (copiable page)   ACTIVITY BANK: *Sex Education*

Activity 18 – Teacher's notes

Who's at risk?

Sexually transmitted infections

AIMS

To reinforce the message that any person who has unprotected sex is at risk of Sexually Transmitted Infections (STIs).
To challenge the stereotypical views some people hold about who is at risk from STIs.

Teaching Points

Materials needed
It may be useful to have leaflets on STIs available or to invite a Health Advisor from your local GU (Genito-Urinary) clinic to talk to pupils.

- Anyone who has unprotected sex is at risk of catching an STI.
- People need to seek medical advice if they think they may have an STI.
- Untreated STIs can have serious long-term effects.
- There is no such thing as safe sex, but using protection during sex is safer.
- Pupils need to take responsibility for their own sexual health.

USING THE ACTIVITY SHEET

The focus of the activity is to convey the strong message that people who have unprotected sex are at risk of catching a sexually transmitted infection.

Step 1 Ask pupils for names of any STIs they have heard of. Write these on the board. Clarify any questions and distribute the leaflets.

Step 2 Place pupils into small groups and ask one pupil in each group to write the following list of categories: teachers, doctors, pop stars, sportspeople, shop assistants, drug misusers, housewives/husbands, bank managers, restaurant owners, middle-aged people, runaways, politicians, prostitutes.

Step 3 Ask groups to discuss what sort of risk factor they feel these categories of people have, in terms of being at risk of catching STIs. Use a scale of 0-7. Draw a table on the board to include the ten categories and a box for the risk factor. Collate and discuss responses.

Step 4 Distribute one blank slip of paper to every pupil. Ask pupils what they think their chances are of catching an STI in the future and to write the number on one side of the paper using the same number scale.

Step 5 Now ask pupils if they think they would ever consider having sex with someone in the future, even a long-term partner, without using a condom. Ask them to write only YES or NO on the other side of the paper. Collect all the slips. Collate the results on the board.

Step 6 Explain the risks of unprotected sex and reflect on and review this information with the results of the exercise.

Step 7 Ask pupils to complete the activity sheet.

Extension Activities

- Hold a class discussion on protection, why many partners leave it to the other person and why it is important to take control of the situation.

Outcomes

- Heightened awareness of the risks associated with having unprotected sex.

Activity Sheet 18

Who's at risk?

It is really important if someone thinks they may have a sexually transmitted infection that they tell their doctor or visit the local GU (Genito-Urinary) clinic. Although it may seem embarrassing, medical staff are used to dealing with such problems. There is no need to be frightened. REMEMBER untreated infections can cause all kinds of problems, such as leaving women unable to have children.

Draw up below some 'golden rules' for protecting yourself against sexually transmitted infections.

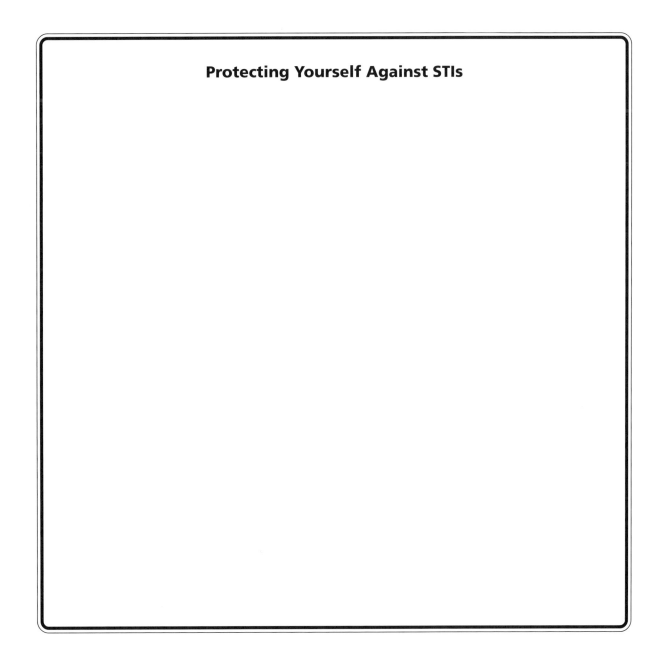

Protecting Yourself Against STIs

There is no such thing as 100% safe sex. There is only safer sex. If someone is sexually active they are at risk of a sexually transmitted disease and unintended pregnancy.

Activity 19 – Teacher's notes

Life choices

Choices that lie ahead in relation to sexual activity

AIMS

To help pupils become aware of the choices that lie ahead of them in relation to their sexual activity.

Teaching Points

- There are many decisions and choices that lie ahead as part of adult life.
- Some of these choices relate to sexual activity.
- It is better to be prepared and ready to make informed choices – through knowledge and understanding – to be as certain as possible that the choice we make is the right choice for us.

USING THE ACTIVITY SHEET

The focus of the activity is to help pupils to think about the choices they will have to make in relation to sexual activity and to help them consider what they really want.

Step 1 Generate with pupils a list of choices that they will make in the future in relation to sexual activity – forming relationships (nature of the relationships, at what age), living with a partner, getting married, remaining celibate (NB young people do not always consider this as one of the choices) or becoming sexually active, practising safer sex, using contraception.

Step 2 Take one of the choices and ask pupils to think of as many pieces of information as they can that would help them to make a choice. For example, what are the consequences of doing or not doing this? What are my religious beliefs? What are my family's beliefs? What are my cultural beliefs? Emphasise to pupils that having as much information as possible about a decision and taking time to consider all aspects of it can help them to make choices they will be happy with.

Step 3 Draw the following diagram on the board, using feedback from the class. Take one of the choices from Step 1 (e.g. becoming sexually active) and write it on the board in a box. Show an arrow from the box leading to another box, to indicate the choice made (e.g. protected sex). Now draw another arrow from the first box to indicate an alternative choice (e.g. unprotected sex). From each new box there may be at least two alternative choices. Continue the diagram until you have exhausted the possibilities.

Step 4 Now ask the pupils, in groups of three, to draw their own diagram on the activity sheet, choosing an example from Step 1. Then ask them to answer the final question on the sheet.

Extension Activities

- Extend the activity by asking pupils to draw two more diagrams individually using different starting points.
- Invite pupils to draw a diagram to show the choices they may decide to make, and share their thoughts with a partner.

Outcomes

- Consideration of the choices that lie ahead.
- Recognising the importance of making responsible and informed choices.

Activity Sheet 19

Life choices

In your groups, take one of the examples from the list of choices and make your own diagram of what could happen.

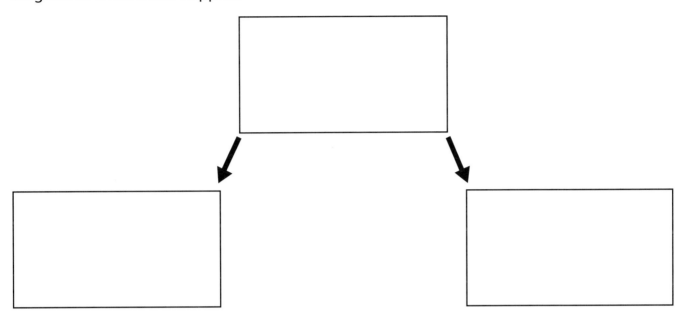

Now write down a piece of advice you would give to someone else when they are trying to make an important life choice.

_____

_____

© Folens (copiable page)   ACTIVITY BANK: *Sex Education*

Activity 20 – Teacher's notes

Dear Exxo Xtra Terrestrial

Clarifying confusions and unanswered questions

AIMS

To deal with any unanswered questions or concerns pupils may have.

Teaching Points

- Exxo (an extraterrestrial being) is a device used to enable pupils to feel more comfortable by using a character as a focus for their questions, rather than directly questioning the teacher.
- The teacher can take on the role of Exxo. Alternatively, this could be a very useful opportunity to bring in the school nurse, health promotion officer or other health professional to answer questions as Exxo.
- If you would like to invite a visitor to take part in this activity, you will need to organise this well in advance.
- If pupils are reluctant to ask questions, it is often helpful to ask them to think of questions someone a little younger than themselves might ask.

USING THE ACTIVITY SHEET

The focus of the activity is to resolve any confusions or questions pupils have and to make this as comfortable as possible by using a fictitious character.

Step 1 Introduce Exxo to the class. Exxo can be a visitor as outlined above, a teacher, a sketch of Exxo or even an empty chair. "Exxo landed on Earth 12 months ago. Its mission was to discover everything there was to find out on Earth about sex and sexuality. Since then it has visited every country and race and gathered a considerable amount of information and is willing to answer any questions you have. If you do not have a question to ask for yourself, think of questions someone a year or two younger than you might ask."

Step 2 Ask pupils (individually or in small groups) to complete the first part of the activity sheet, writing down three questions.

Step 3 Now ask pupils to write one of the questions on a slip of paper, anonymously. Collect all the slips and pass them to Exxo to answer or answer them as Exxo. Visitors (and teachers) sometimes like to see the questions beforehand, so you could do the first part of this activity in preparation for the next session.

Step 4 In pairs or groups, ask pupils to write a very short letter to Exxo asking it for some advice on a sexual matter. Pupils write the letter on the activity sheet.

Step 5 Pass the letter to another pair or group, asking them to write a short reply in the space provided on the activity sheet.

Step 6 Review by asking random groups to read out their letters and replies.

Extension Activities

- Invite pupils to compile the letters and replies into a problem page – involve the IT Department.
- Use Exxo in other PSHE lessons – it could answer questions in a similar way on drug-related issues.

Outcomes

- Clarification of any outstanding questions and issues.
- Problem-solving skill development.

Activity Sheet 20

Dear Exxo Xtra Terrestrial

What three questions would you like to ask Exxo?

1. _____

2. _____

3. _____

Dear Exxo,

Dear Writer,

© Folens (copiable page)   ACTIVITY BANK: *Sex Education*   43

Activity 21 – Teacher's notes

Who's out there?

Where to go for help and advice

AIMS

To raise awareness of who is available if pupils need help and advice.

Teaching Points

Materials needed
Video resource from GU or Family Planning clinic (optional).

- At this stage in their lives, pupils will not need very detailed information, but will benefit from discussion about how to ask for help and what the key contact places might be.
- If pupils have previously completed Activity 20, they will have generated a number of questions that could be used within this activity to consider who you would approach to ask which question.
- It can be useful to invite a Family Planning Nurse or Doctor and/or Health Advisor from the local GU (Genito-Urinary) clinic to talk to pupils about their perceptions (NB organise well in advance).
- Remind pupils that using the biological language for sexual organs can help them to feel less embarrassed when asking a question and also means they can be clearly understood.

USING THE ACTIVITY SHEET

The focus of the activity is to raise awareness of the people and agencies who can offer support and help in relation to sexual health matters.

Step 1 Refer the class to the activity sheet which shows a range of people who can offer help and support. Discuss with the class the kinds of issues they would approach each one with, what would be difficult to discuss with some people and what would be easy.

Step 2 Discuss with the class their perceptions of visiting the doctor – does it feel comfortable, friendly? Is the doctor helpful? What do they think it would be like visiting a Family Planning clinic? Genito-Urinary clinic? Is it different for boys and girls? If so, why is this?

Some Family Planning services and GU clinics have videos showing aspects of their work. This may be a useful point at which to play one or alternatively an appropriate time to invite one of the health professionals mentioned previously into the classroom.

Step 3 Invite pupils to complete the activity sheet by writing where they would go or who they would approach with each issue.

Step 4 Review by asking pupils to share the answers on their activity sheet.

Extension Activities

- Many GU and Family Planning clinics will arrange a visit and talk for school parties or pupils can write to them asking for details about their work.
- Invite pupils to compile an information sheet giving details of where to go for help with contact addresses and telephone numbers – the English and IT Departments may help.

Outcomes

- Raised awareness of the key contact points for support.
- Reinforcement of the usefulness of using correct biological language.

Activity Sheet 21

Who's out there?

Who can I ask for help about sexual matters?

Family Planning clinic

Genito-Urinary clinic

Teacher

Parents or carers

School nurse

GP

Friend

Who would you approach to discuss the following issues?

Contraception _____

Your sexual feelings about someone else _____

Discomfort on passing urine _____

Concerns you have because you have had unprotected sex _____

A friend who you suspect might be pregnant _____

Concerns you have about an aspect of your sexual development _____

Other pupils ridiculing you and calling you names in relation to your sexuality _____

Severe itching in your genital area _____

© Folens (copiable page) ACTIVITY BANK: *Sex Education*

Appendix

Additional information for 'Knowing the facts' (pages 28–29)

Male

Penis	Usually soft and limp. When sexually aroused, an increase in blood flow makes it go stiff and hard and stand up erect so that it can fit into a female's vagina.
Testis	One of a pair of testes which make sperm cells.
Scrotum	A sac containing the two testes.
Bladder	Stores urine.
Foreskin	Protects the sensitive part of the penis which is called the glans. The glans is the tip of the penis. Jewish and Muslim boys do not have foreskins. These are removed when they are babies. A small number of boys are also circumcised for non-religious reasons.
Sperm duct	Carries sperm away from testes.
Epididymis	Sometimes called the sperm store. A small coiled tube lying behind each testis.

Female

Vagina	The opening leading to the internal sex organs. Blood passes out of this opening during a period. The opening is able to stretch to accommodate a penis during sex or a baby's head during childbirth.
Labia	The outer labia are the outer lips of the vagina which close around the inner labia and protect the other external sex organs. The inner labia are two thin delicate folds of skin which are very sensitive when touched.
Clitoris	A small pea-like structure amongst the inner labia. A very sensitive organ.
Urethra	The opening through which a female passes urine.
Anus	The back opening through which faeces are excreted.

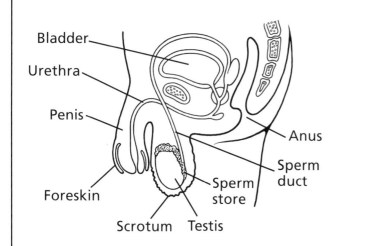
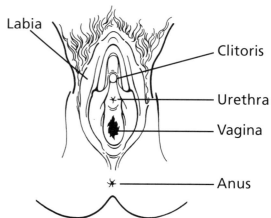

Statements for 'Stepping into their shoes' (pages 22–23)

a. People should not have sex before they are married to each other.
b. If everyone was taught how to use condoms properly it would help to stop the spread of HIV.
c. People should just be left to make their own choices about sex – it's up to them.
d. I'm very worried that more and more under 16s seem to be given contraceptives without their parents knowing.
e. Boys just don't take an equal share of responsibility when it comes to practising safer sex.
f. Alcohol is responsible for a lot of young people becoming sexually active before they are really ready.
g. I wish we could find a way of convincing girls that if they have sex at too young an age they have a significant risk of getting cancer of the cervix later on.
h. Sex is a very natural thing to do. I don't know why people make so much fuss about safer sex.
i. It's no good telling us just to say no! You don't know what it's like to be teased by your mates because you're still a virgin. It's humiliating.
j. I wish I had waited, but how was I to know that at 15?

Additional information for 'What language shall we use?' (pages 30–31)

To the teacher: explain to parents that you are about to begin a series of sex education lessons and outline the topics you will be covering. Photocopy this list of terminology and explain that these words will be used in class and that parents may want to discuss them with their children before the class. You may also like to enclose the diagrams of the male and female genital anatomy (see page 46) for further preparation.

Some useful sexual terminology

Petting	Partners touching and exploring each other prior to, or instead of, sexual intercourse.
Sexual intercourse	The insertion of the penis into the vagina.
Wet dreams	During puberty, boys can experience semen leaking from the penis when they are asleep.
Ejaculation	At the point of orgasm in the male, semen spurts from the penis.
Virgin	Someone who has not experienced sexual intercourse.
Semen	Thick, whitish mixture of sperm and fluid which comes out of the penis when the male has an orgasm or 'comes'.
Orgasm	The peak of sexual excitement which gives a feeling of pleasure.
Erection	When a male is sexually aroused the penis becomes stiff and hard.
Homosexual	People who are sexually attracted to someone of the same sex as themselves.
Masturbation	Touching or stroking of one's own sex organs.

Additional information for 'What have you heard?' (pages 36–37)

1. The only possible routes of transmission are blood, sexual secretions (semen and vaginal secretions) and mother's milk. If none of these are involved, HIV infection will not be transmitted.
2. HIV cannot be passed on from social contact like touching, hugging and kissing, sharing use of cups and cutlery or from toilet seats.
3. HIV causes damage to the body's defence system.
4. People with HIV can stay healthy for many years. However, they may develop illnesses because of their infection. These may only be successfully treated if they are caught early enough.
5. AIDS stands for Acquired Immune Deficiency Syndrome. This is a medical term for people who are HIV positive and develop particular illnesses due to their damaged defence system.

This information is taken from a leaflet, *HIV and AIDS Drug Abuse*, produced by The Standing Conference on Drug Abuse (SCODA).

Skills matrix

ACTIVITY/SKILL	1	2	3	4	5	6	7	8	9	10	11	12	13	14	15	16	17	18	19	20	21
Analysing/Interpreting		●		●		●	●	●	●	●	●				●	●			●		●
Asserting									●		●										
Awareness	●		●	●	●	●			●	●	●		●	●	●	●	●	●	●	●	●
Collating	●													●		●			●		●
Communicating	●	●	●	●	●	●	●	●	●	●	●	●	●		●	●	●	●	●	●	●
Comparing		●	●	●	●	●	●		●	●	●	●	●	●	●	●			●		●
Cooperating		●												●							
Debating and discussing		●	●	●	●	●	●	●	●	●	●	●	●	●	●	●			●	●	●
Decision making				●			●	●		●			●		●		●		●		
Empathising			●			●		●	●	●	●										
Evaluating		●	●	●	●	●	●	●	●	●	●	●	●	●	●	●	●	●	●		●
Expressing (e.g. of beliefs, ideas and opinions)		●	●	●	●	●	●	●	●	●	●	●	●	●	●	●			●	●	
ICT																				●	●
Identity and self-esteem			●		●	●		●	●	●	●								●		
Imagining				●		●	●	●		●		●			●						
Investigating									●	●						●				●	●
Knowledge	●		●	●	●				●				●	●	●	●	●	●	●	●	●
Listening			●			●	●	●	●	●	●	●			●						
Negotiating		●							●	●											
Perceiving			●			●		●		●	●			●	●			●	●		●
Presenting			●				●	●	●	●		●				●				●	
Prioritising								●											●		
Problem solving									●			●								●	●
Respect			●	●		●				●	●						●		●		
Responsibility							●	●					●		●				●	●	●
Understanding	●	●	●	●	●	●	●	●	●	●	●	●	●	●	●	●	●	●	●	●	●